TABLE OF CONTENTS

CHAPTER 1

LAND OF FJORDS

Bergen is one of northern Europe's oldest **ports**. Fishermen have been selling their catch here since 1276! This port is in Norway. It is filled with colorful buildings. Welcome!

Bergen

Norway has more **fjords** than any other country. There are more than 1,000 here! Sognefjord is the longest. It is 127 miles (204 kilometers) long.

Sognefjord

Trolltunga

Mountains and other rock **formations** fill the land. One is called Trolltunga. It means "troll tongue." People hike to this cliff. It sits about 2,300 feet (700 meters) above Lake Ringedalsvatnet.

DID YOU KNOW?

Glaciers formed the fjords. They created valleys as they moved across the land.

A train ride is a good way to see this beautiful country. The Flåm Railway travels about 12.5 miles (20 km) between Flåm and Myrdal. Travelers can see mountains covered in snow. They see rivers and waterfalls.

Flåm
Railway

CHAPTER 2

TROLLS AND TRADITIONS

Norwegian **myths** tell stories of trolls. These creatures make trouble in forests and mountains. They are not real. But you can see statues of them here!

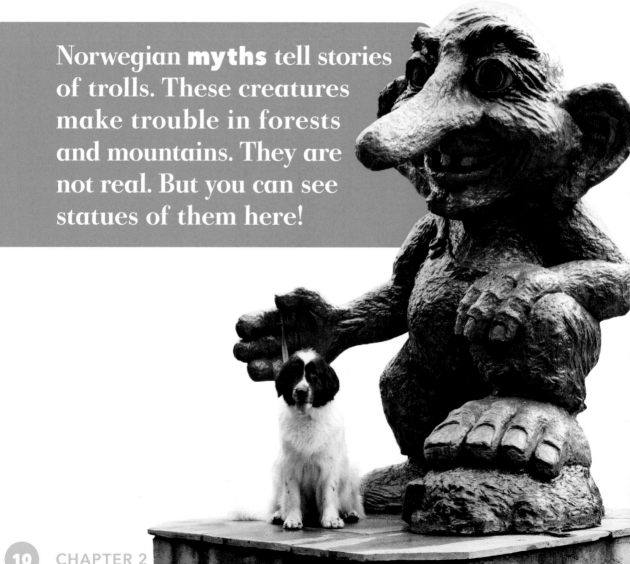

krumkake

A Christmas **tradition** is making different kinds of cookies. Krumkake is one. It is a thin, rolled cookie. People use irons to stamp patterns on them.

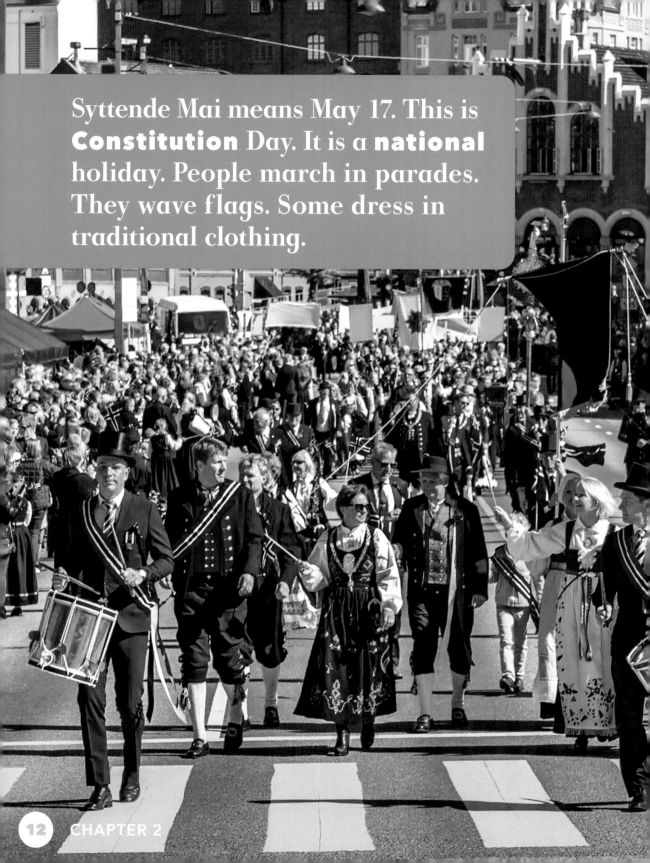

Syttende Mai means May 17. This is **Constitution** Day. It is a **national** holiday. People march in parades. They wave flags. Some dress in traditional clothing.

TAKE A LOOK!

The bunad is the traditional Norwegian outfit. What are the parts called? Take a look!

HEADDRESS

HAT

JEWELRY

JACKET

BLOUSE

VEST

BELT

SKIRT

TROUSERS

APRON

STOCKING

CHAPTER 3

LIFE IN NORWAY

Oslo is Norway's largest city. It is also the **capital**. A **monarch** chooses a prime minister. The prime minister leads the government.

Oslo

Part of Norway is in the Arctic Circle. Arctic animals live throughout the country. Reindeer and elk are common. Wolverines and lemmings live here, too.

reindeer

Children learn Norwegian at home. They start learning English in second grade. Students who complete high school may go to college. Others begin working.

Many people in Norway work in the oil business. Others build ships. Some people make paper products. Fishing is another important job.

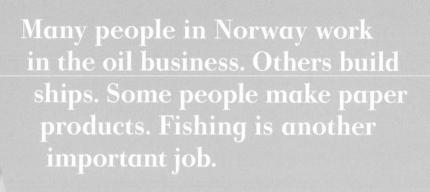

WHAT DO YOU THINK?

Why do you think fishing is important in Norway? What jobs do people have where you live?

Before people here had cars, they traveled by skis! Now skiing is the national sport. Kids learn to ski before they are old enough to go to school! Many towns have ski jumps.

Norway is a beautiful country. Do you want to visit?

WHAT DO YOU THINK?

Norway's **climate** is mild. It snows in winter. During summer, the sun shines 24 hours a day in the north. What is the climate like where you live?

QUICK FACTS & TOOLS

Norwegian Sea

Arctic Circle

SWEDEN

NORWAY

FINLAND

RUSSIA

Flåm • Myrdal
Bergen •
★ Oslo

North Sea

N
W ╋ E
S

NORWAY

Location: northern Europe

Size: 148,726 square miles
(385,199 square kilometers)

Population: 5,467,439
(July 2020 estimate)

Capital: Oslo

Type of Government: parliamentary
constitutional monarchy

Languages: Norwegian, Sami

Exports: petroleum products,
paper products, machinery,
metals, ships, fish

Currency: kroner

capital: A city where government leaders meet.

climate: The weather typical of a certain place over a long period of time.

constitution: The basic laws of a country that state the rights of the people and the powers of the government.

formations: Structures or arrangements of something.

fjords: Long, narrow inlets of the ocean between high cliffs.

glaciers: Very large, slow-moving masses of ice.

monarch: A person who rules a country, such as a king or queen.

myths: Old stories that express the beliefs or history of a group of people.

national: Of, having to do with, or shared by a whole nation.

ports: Towns or cities with harbors where ships can load and unload goods.

tradition: A custom, idea, or belief that is handed down from one generation to the next.

Norway's currency

INDEX

TO LEARN MORE

Finding more information is as easy as 1, 2, 3.

1. **Go to www.factsurfer.com**
2. **Enter "Norway" into the search box.**
3. **Choose your book to see a list of websites.**

FACT SURFER